HALCYON DAYS OF BUSES

Front cover, top: A Roe-bodied AEC Regent owned by Baillie Bros of Dumbarton, complete with an AEC-Ricardo 8.8litre oil engine, passing Kelvin Hall, Glasgow in 1934.

Front cover, bottom: New in April 1933 to Weald of Kent, of Tenterden, this Thornycroft Cygnet with Strachans bodywork, was acquired by Maidstone and District in November of the same year. It is seen here at Victoria before transfer of the authorised terminal from Eccleston Bridge to Victoria Coach Station.

Back cover, top: A postwar scene at Worcester with both South Midland and Midland Red vehicles mainly on express services to London and the south.

Back cover, bottom: Wartime mixture. This 1937 Bristol GO5G, new to Brighton Hove and District with convertible open-top bodywork, was loaned to United Counties between 1942 and 1944.

South Wales operators were influenced by diesel engines on the basis that fuel could be obtained from locally produced coal. Little happened in that direction but KG 3708, a Cardiff Corporation AEC Regent bodied by Northern Counties which was delivered in 1934 had an 8.8litre oil engine. It was the first of 10 such buses delivered that year although a demonstrator had been acquired previously.

HALCYON DAYS OF BUSES

J.F.Parke & A.J.Francis

LONDON
IAN ALLAN LTD

First published 1983

ISBN 0 7110 1325 X

Published by Ian Allan Ltd,
Shepperton, Surrey; and printed by
Ian Allan Printing Ltd at their works
at Coombelands in Runnymede,
England

All the photographs in this book were taken
from the Charles F. Klapper collection of the
Omnibus Society but kind acknowledgements
should be made for the use of certain pictures
from AEC, Leyland Motors, Thornycroft,
Burrow's Newspapers and Cooper & Son,
Northampton. The authors would also like to
thank Reg Durrant, Brodie Jackson, Alan
Nightingale and Terence Uden for their
assistance in compiling this album and in
particular Eileen Klapper for ensuring the
photographs and negatives were most carefully
looked after and Sylvia Francis for her
considerable patience in typing the script.

J. F. Park
A. J. Franci
London, January 198

This page: Shrewsbury Barker Street bus station during
World War 2. An SOS IM4 of 1932 with Brush body
loads in front of a SON of the 1937 series with English
Electric body. After the war the bus station was relocated
to an alternative site in Barker Street.

Contents

Charles F. Klapper
FCIT, FRGS

Charles F. Klapper, a founder member of the Omnibus Society and for some years editor of *Modern Transport*, amassed a comprehensive collection of transport photographs covering the period from the mid-1920s until the early 1970s. He took the majority of these photographs himself. While his interests included all modes and aspects of transport, he will be best remembered for his many books and articles on road and rail history.

On his death a good deal of the material was left to the Omnibus Society and it was felt that a selection should be published in album form in memory to the invaluable work carried out by Charles in recording the many transport developments of his time. Such a publication would also give transport enthusiasts an opportunity to see some unpublished material of the past.

Charles, a true Londoner, born within the sound of Bow Bells, was educated at Coopers' Company School, leaving there in 1924 to be employed first by a haulage contractor, Capon & Son. Eight years later he went to work for his brother's printing firm in the Mile End Road. It was shortly before this, in 1929, that Charles, together with a number of transport enthusiasts created the Omnibus Society. Charles became its first secretary and remained so until 1946.

Meanwhile in 1934 Charles left the family firm and for a few months was assistant editor to a trade magazine *Furniture Manufacturer*. In 1935 he was fortunate enough to obtain an appointment as an editorial assistant with the weekly newspaper, *Modern Transport,* or 'The Times of the Transport World'.

The next year he joined the Institute of Transport as a graduate and with war coming not long afterwards the opportunity for promotion arose. From January 1941 the then editor of *Modern Transport*, David Lamb, was seconded to the Ministry of Food as Deputy Director of Food Transport. As a consequence, Charles became acting editor and remained so for the remainder of the war, writing over 200 leading articles during this time.

After the war, Charles resumed the role of assistant editor, but soon afterwards became editor and subsequently a director with *Modern Transport* until his retirement in 1970, by which time *Modern Transport* had turned to consultancy. His interests in the Omnibus Society, as with other organisations, were extensive and long enduring. After leaving as secretary with 17 years service, he became Chairman for the 1947-48 session and President in 1950. He was later appointed a vice-president and from time to time wrote papers on a variety of subjects although often concentrating on the London scene with which he was most familiar. His connection with the Institute of Transport was also noteworthy. He was chairman of its Metropolitan Graduate and Student Society and later, following its postwar reconstitution, a chairman of its Metropolitan Section. He delivered a Henry Spurrier Memorial Lecture, served also as a vice-president and was closely concerned in wartime and postwar development of postal tutorial courses.

The Bus Business

This album portrays something of the bus scene during the three decades, starting in 1930, when public road transport was consolidating after a rapid growth period, although it was still an expanding industry. Since the pictures are drawn from a personal collection, comprehensive coverage of the whole of the British Isles may not be achieved totally. Some areas were photographed in particular depth and certain operators were the subject of detailed examination in the pages of *Modern Transport*. It is the material collected on these investigations which has been drawn upon to compile this reflection upon those halcyon days.

Although the railways dominated the transport business until World War 1, allowing many people a high degree of mobility, a large proportion of the population did not require intensive or extensive transport facilities. Frequently home, workplace and such social activities as were available, could be found in close proximity. The tramcar, mainly in its electric form and later the motor vehicle, began to change the whole life style of the community.

The bus, for example, could offer increased convenience with greater flexibility than the railway or tram networks. Capital investment in buses was much lower than these other systems and in many cases extensive bus networks could be provided at relatively low cost. This afforded the majority of the population a higher standard of mobility than had been achieved before, with access to additional work opportunities and recreational activities. Many rural areas were provided with their first ever public transport links to neighbouring villages and towns. As public transport was a growth industry, many operators offered a wide range of services, some of which, especially in the rural areas, operated at a loss. These losses were cross subsidised by well patronised urban and inter-urban operations. The whole of the bus industry was largely self-supporting and indeed was a successful commercial enterprise, providing a necessary social service.

There were some problems nevertheless; World War 2 intervened; competition within the industry, albeit of benefit to the consumer, produced headaches. Labour relations difficulties caused some occasional damaging strikes, showing that despite the population's high degree of reliance on buses, life could continue at least for a time without them. Nevertheless, until the latter part of the 1950s the market for bus travel was secure and few operators had real worries about making ends meet.

Most local and many longer journeys were reliant on the bus; travel to and from work, trips to the shops, cinema, theatre and visits to relations. The alternatives were often to cycle or walk. Behind the mantelpiece would be the local bus timetable. Just after World War 2, buses held some 40% of the passenger business and cycling around 10%. Private transport accounted for 30% and railways the remainder. Buses were a cornerstone of social life at virtually all levels.

Today the motor car has become the dominant form of inland transport, but in 1930, the same year that saw the passing of the Road Traffic Act which introduced the first comprehensive control on the bus business, there were only just over one million motor cars and light vans. During the remainder of that decade, these rose to nearly one and a half million in number, falling rapidly to half that total during the war years with petrol rationing and restrictions on travel. How matters altered once postwar prosperity and rationing disappeared! By 1960 cars numbered over 12 million — an increase of some 1,200% since 1930. Driving licences had gone up from 2.9 million to 10 million over the same three decades.

Changes in the social life of the population also affected the fortunes of the bus business by the time 1960 was reached. Many of the highly populated areas of the inner cities were removed and the creation of new low density housing became a mixed blessing. All too often poor planning of road layouts and the location of houses left the bus at a disadvantage in no longer being able to provide an attractively routed, economical and frequent service. Television quickly took over from the cinema and attendances at some spectator sports declined as home entertainment found a foothold.

Fortunately, although debates continued about the precise level and method of financial support now necessary to sustain a comprehensive bus network, the importance of maintaining public transport is realised. Over half the population does not have regular access to private transport and there is a need to offer an alternative to the car as a means of enhancing the quality of life, especially in urban areas. There are also plenty of signs that the business-like skills found in the developing and halcyon days of buses live on.

The leaders of the industry throughout the period covered by this book were in most cases the first generation of busmen, gradually succeeded by the next — all were personalities and characters. Arther Henry Hawkins, who having built up the East Surrey business went on to manage, autocratically, the Country Bus and Coach Department of London Transport until the end of the war. He was succeeded by Brian Harbour, who went on to become a member of London Transport Executive and in turn was succeeded by Geoffrey Fernyhough who maintained a very high esprit de corps among the staff. As a result a first class level of service was maintained.

Although wellknown even today, Frank Pick, who retired in 1940, was one of the main instrumentalists in creating a second to none passenger transport system in London and devoted his life to the industry and built foundations which last for all time. In the provinces, the Tilling organisation and its subsidiaries were controlled centrally under the leadership of accountant Frederick Heaton whose main preoccupation was the maintenance of a profitable business. British Electric Traction (BET) equally prosperous, was far more decentralised and under Sidney Garcke allowed local managers greater freedom in decision making. In these opening words it is only possible to mention a few of the many, but for them all, none of the delights we now look upon would have taken place.

Reference has been made to Tilling and BET, which together with the railways owned the majority of the larger provincial bus companies. These had area agreements defining operating territory, providing the opportunity for planned expansion and then consolidation. Up to 1930 this was hampered by the absence of a uniform system of control or licensing. Competition from independent operators produced short term benefits for passengers in the form of lower fares and higher frequencies, but such situations hampered long term security. For example, insufficient cash was being earned in some situations for asset replacement and the maintenance of many remote rural services.

The 1930 Road Traffic Act, born out of a Royal Commission on Transport, introduced a strict control of both the quantity, in the form of licences for all regular bus and coach services, and quality, by licensing drivers and conductors and requiring the regular examination of vehicles. Although also used to provide the railways with some protection against the advances of road transport, the Act produced a measure of order and continuity.

The bus industry grew because of a demand

for personal mobility, the interruption in the growth of private transport during the war and also because it took over from many tram networks in urban areas. During the 1920s there were over 14,000 tramcars, mainly in municipal ownership. This had diminished by half during the 1930s and by 1960 had disappeared almost entirely. Leyland Motors advised operators to bury their trams and buy Titans — the revolutionary double-decker introduced in 1928.

This vehicle incorporating a lowheight body, increased flexibility of operation and safety was an example of how the industry was able to maintain business on a firm basis during the next three decades. AEC produced its rival Regent range and manufacturers such as Bedford (Vauxhall Motors) introduced in 1931 the benefits of mass production with the small WHB and WLB models, ideal for low cost rural operation. From these evolved the OB model, introduced in 1938 and applicable for both a 29-seat coach body or a slightly higher capacity bus body. This remained in production until 1950 and during the war over 3,300 chassis were produced (designated OWB), fulfilling a vital need to restock and supplement many fleets at this crucial time.

While many tram undertakings turned to the motor bus, trolleybuses also became a familiar form of public transport. In 1936 a total of 26 local authorities and five companies, as well as London Transport, operated 1,600 trolleybuses and over 500 were on order. They were chosen since much of the tramway capital infrastructure, such as power stations and overhead traction wiring could be used, which still had much life left.

While the 1930s saw the continued use of petrol, the oil engine, offering increased reliability and economy, was becoming popular.

With the main exception of the side-engined AEC Q and the Northern General SE6, it was not until postwar that anything other than a front-engined vehicle was generally available. Coming at a time when the permitted length of a vehicle was increased from 27ft 6in (8.4m) to 30ft (9m), the underfloor-engined chassis enabled a higher carrying capacity to be achieved. Names such as the Leyland Royal Tiger, now recently revived, became commonplace during the 1950s. Such vehicles allowed the subsequent growth of one-man operation, necessary to combat the early effects of traffic loss, since for most of the three decades nearly all buses and some coaches had both a driver and a conductor.

Fare collection in prewar days involved preprinted punch tickets with firms such as Bell Punch, Williamson and the Glasgow Numerical Printing Company providing much of the necessary material. Ticket machines appeared quite early with, for example, the Bellgraphic on which the conductor wrote the fare paid, with a carbon copy taken to record the transaction. The TIM machine was one of the earliest machines which printed tickets from a paper roll, while the Setright company developed first an 'insert' model which recorded fare details on preprinted tickets, and later a machine which needed only a plain roll. In these pages we have displayed some examples of interesting tickets, from that time when machines had not taken over entirely.

The authors hope that some of the atmosphere of the period is conveyed and that the photographs and other material chosen, such as timetables, provide a cross-section of the industry from the decade when some consolidation was taking place, through the turbulent war years until the time when traffic began significantly to decline.

Salad Days for London Transport

A need to co-ordinate the planning and running of public transport in the capital had been apparent for many years although it took an unusual partnership of a Labour Minister of Transport, Herbert Morrison, and Lord Ashfield, private enterprise champion and chairman of the Underground group, to take the necessary initial steps. London Transport, an independent self-supporting organisation emerged in the summer of 1933 which, in return for a virtual total monopoly, set high standards of service.

LT in the 1930s could best be remembered for the consolidation of its territory with route reorganisations to incorporate the many acquired independent services as well as the further development of standard vehicle designs already the practice of the London General Company. Trolleybuses took over from some trams, but World War 2 interrupted plans and while bringing additional business, also brought the well-recorded additional problems of enemy action and vehicle shortages. Prestige Green Line services came and went during this period but by the late forties and the next decade, LT was emerging as a highly standardised and organised concern, able and willing to operate an efficient and intensive network of bus services from Baldock in the north to Crawley in the south and westwards from Grays to Windsor.

Most coach operators in London, however, escaped take-over and a small number of operators such as Birch Brothers continued unscathed to run a limited number of stage service within LT's area.

Right: ST 889 an ex-Tilling vehicle, new in August 1930, is seen here in London Transport livery on route 1, by Somerset House. These vehicles were given an extended life because of the war with many loaned to the provinces.

Left: A scene in 1931 in General days at Bromley North with LT1077 on route 609 to Penge via Westmoreland Road, which started in April of that year and is now served by route 126 also, currently, single-deck operated. The 35-seat AEC Renown vehicle is seen in 'as new' condition having been delivered a month after route 609 commenced.

Below: Another Bromley view, but this time postwar, with LT1181 on 227 having turned out of Beckenham Lane into the High Street, bound for Chislehurst. A newly-delivered RT is behind on route 47.

Above: Rear ends, wartime style, at the Clapham
Common Old Town terminus. Open staircase LT35, built
in 1931, is on route 35 while the seven years younger
STL2495 is working 45.

Below: London Bridge station with LT1250 on route 17
to Shepherds Bush via Oxford Circus and Notting Hill
Gate, a service withdrawn in August 1958 after
the effects of the long bus strike that year, which reduced
passenger traffic dramatically.

Above left: Before the war, London Transport only purchased AEC double-deckers, with the exception of 100 Leyland Titan TD4s classified STD which were allocated to Hendon garage. STD88 passes Burnt Oak station on 52 in September 1939, prior to the application of blackout specification.

Below left: B4 (FXT 422) a Bristol K5G with Park Royal bodywork was one of nine 'unfrozen' chassis allocated to London Transport in 1942. It was employed initially on route 97 (Brentford-Greenford), working out of Hanwell Garage when this picture was taken. Later, Bristols delivered to London Transport towards the end of the war had the more modern PV2 radiator and AEC 7.7litre engines.

Below: Morden station in July 1940 with STL1156 on a short route 50 to Raynes Park. Note the extensive destination blind information for what was a relative short distance service. Route 50 commenced in February 1939 and had been withdrawn by early 1942, being replaced by an extension of 118.

Above right: With some windows boarded up, lowbridge STL1617 built in 1936, but with wartime bodywork, stands at the route 230 terminus at Northwick Park, before departing for Rayners Lane. This vehicle was one of four sent to Harrow Weald in 1942 for this route, replacing single-deck Q type buses.

Right: Allocated to Merton and on the terminal stand at Oxford Circus, D181 represents some of the many utility vehicles acquired by London Transport. The vehicle, a Daimler CWD6 with Duple body had its Daimler engine replaced in 1950 by an AEC one. Note the conductress talking to the driver, also representing the many women employed to replace the men who had joined the Forces. The rather drab dust coat was typical uniform for the time.

Below: The rear-engined Leyland Cubs, made up of 48 production vehicles and one prototype were delivered at the outbreak of the war and although intended to augment the small Central Bus one-man-operated vehicle fleet, were put into store. After a time some were used as peak hour relief buses as seen here with CR28 on route 73.

Above left: This utility Guy Arab I with body by Park Royal, G4, arrived in London during February 1943 and was allocated to Tottenham. On a grey day after hostilities had ceased, it waits at Liverpool Street, providing a peak hour journey on route 76.

Above right: After the rush hour, postwar style, on route 96 (Wanstead-Putney Common) in the Strand. This service was another victim of the 1958 bus strike, being withdrawn in August of that year. STL234, delivered in October 1933 was originally petrol engined with a Daimler pre-selector gearbox. An oil engine was fitted later.

Below: Morden station with a single-deck LT on route 245 bound for South Wimbledon (via Cheam and New Malden) and another view of route 50 with STL631 heading for Raynes Park. Both services were mainly feeder routes for the Underground.

Above: Greenwich Church with
STL1672 working tram replacement
route 163 introduced in July 1952
between Plumstead Common and the
Embankment, taking over the tram
route 40 (Woolwich-Embankment).
The bus stop advertises Sunday bus
excursions, which, while restricted to
the London Transport area, proved
popular with Londoners at a time
when private motoring was not
available generally.

Right: STL1310 in Pickhurst Lane,
Hayes on the Bromley-Coney Hall
service 138, during the late 1940s with
a total absence of traffic.

Above left: London borrowed buses from the provinces on a number of occasions during the 1940s. This Leeds Corporation AEC Regent, ANW 674, one of 17 such vehicles sent to Bromley waits at Coney Hall immediately after the war on route 138 from Bromley.

Left: Modern vehicles at last! Some early deliveries of RTLs went to Sidcup Garage as shown by RTL9 at Finsbury Square with another example in the background. An LT in its last days can be seen on route 43.

Below: London's premier services seen at the Law Courts with an RT on route 9 and an STL on 11, both bound for Liverpool Street, highlighting the period during the late 1940s when new and old rubbed shoulders for a while.

Right: Stratford Broadway with an RTW on route 32 which commenced in August 1959 between Victoria and Wanstead, replacing trolleybus route 661, between Aldgate and Leyton.

London's Trolleybuses

This was the largest trolleybus network in the world, rising to a maximum of over 1,700 vehicles, replacing tram services mainly in North and East London.

Below: Stamford Hill with No 980, an AEC664T trolleybus of the J2 class. This was the exchange point between the 649 trolleybus service (which was running between Ponders End and Stamford Hill) and the 49 tram service which continued through to Liverpool Street. This arrangement lasted between October 1938 and February 1939 when the trolleybus was extended to replace totally the tram service.

Above: DLY 708, an all-Leyland vehicle, passing the Acton tram depot, one of the premises of the London United Tramways network, which was used for a short while by trolleybuses, before finally closing in 1936.

Left: Aldgate terminus with AEC FXH 613 on route 663 to Ilford. For a few months it was extended through to Chadwell Heath. It was withdrawn in August 1959.

Above: Another view of Aldgate with operating staff looking on at roadworks, together with a route 653 trolleybus. As seen here, this was the terminus of a number of frequent Green Line services to Upminster and Brentwood, now either withdrawn or much curtailed although more sensibly the one remaining service from Grays is extended to Victoria.

The Country Area

Below: Interchange early postwar style at Westerham. O 410 for Reigate is a loaned Bristol K5G from United Automobile, while in the Bromley direction, heads 'Godstone', STL1049; an RT, is ready to leave for Croydon and Wallington; in the distance T609 has arrived on Green Line 706 from Aylesbury and is headin for its terminus at Westerham Station. Such interchang arrangements still continue today, although without the presence of Green Line which is restricted to Sundays only.

Above: Our brief review of London's Country buses starts in 1931 with this East Surrey AEC Provincial S type vehicle on route 410 bound for Reigate, at the Bromley North station terminus. This was one year before the short lived London General Country Services was formed and the last days of open top bus operation on such services. More modern vehicles are typified by KR 3892 a Ransomes-bodied AEC Regent also owned by East Surrey, seen in the background. This was one of four similar buses which came from the associated undertaking, Autocar Services of Tunbridge Wells which found them surplus to the number for which it could obtain licences.

Below: Amersham was one of the new garages built by London Transport and opened in 1935 to replace the adjacent premises of Amersham & District. This view includes an ex-Skylark Gilford (GF127) furthest from the camera and UU 6640 (T25), an AEC Regal which originated from the LGOC in 1929 as part of an initial batch of 49 vehicles. This particular vehicle was transferred to East Surrey and in due course to the Country Bus Department. HV 66 (R42) was an AEC Reliance acquired from Battens, which was operating an Aldgate-Tilbury service.

Above: TF37 when new in May 1939. One of 75 similar vehicles delivered that year to augment the Green Line fleet and initially all allocated to Romford garage (RE).

Right: Some vehicles were converted to gas producer operation to conserve liquid fuels. This AEC Regal, T355, was new to Queen Line but rebodied by Weymann in 1935. It was disposed of to the War Department for the Control Commission in Germany in 1945.

Below right: Green Line services were suspended during the war but then reinstated for a period. Many of the coaches had meanwhile been converted to ambulances and during this period some double-deck buses were employed which served also to reduce the need for duplication which was rarely practicable in any case. STL1150 is operating route 33 (Oxford Circus-High Wycombe) which started in December 1940 but was withdrawn in 1942.

Left: London General Country Services at Reigate ordered 12 lowbridge AEC Regents which were delivered to London Transport in April and May 1934. They became known as the Godstone STLs. Since the Reigate office was headquarters of the Country Bus Department, Surrey registrations were applied. Bodywork for these buses was by Weymann and, an unusual practice for that time, doors were fitted. Pictured is STL1048 (BPF 289) at Limpsfield running from Godstone on route 410 (Bromley-Reigate). These vehicles lasted until 1952.

Below left: The Leyland Cub was introduced in 1935 and replaced many of the small vehicles acquired from various independent operators. The Country Bus model, of which there were 74, had 4.4litre diesel engines and Short Bros 20-seat bodywork. Together with their Central Bus counterparts which were fitted with slightly larger 4.7litre engines, they became a standard small bus of LPTB and remained the only one-man-operated vehicles in the fleet until the GS arrived in 1953 to replace them. C61 is shown at Westerham loading for a Sunday afternoon departure on the 465 to Edenbridge. This route was never busy except for leisure traffic as is seen here. It is still maintained, although now on a joint basis by an independent and Maidstone & District.

A Few Independents

Right: It was not unusual for housebuilders to offer free bus services, prior to the provision of conventional services by the major operators. This is Hayes Station in 1935 with a Leyland Cub on Morrells operation to the Coney Hall Estate, now served by LT route 138.

Above: United Service Transport, formed in 1919 to take over the old-established Balham firm of French's Garage and Motor Works, had a fleet of some 400 freight vehicles engaged on contract work. Its coaches worked seasonal services from South London to seaside resorts, undertook contract work for airlines and much private hire. A party of ramblers is seen with the 1934 AEC Regal with Harrington body which had taken them to the Surrey village of Hascombe.

Right: The bull's eye sign on the bus stop is no more in Edenbridge and neither is London Country, as successor to London Transport. However, this Gilford, belonging to J. Sargent of East Grinstead and previously Thackray's Way was working on a service acquired by Southdown in 1951. It was passed on to Maidstone & District almost immediately afterwards.

Below right: An independent on the fringe of the LT area at Windsor. Borough Services operated a 30-minute frequency between the town and Clewer Green, before the route later passed to Thames Valley.

Left: This Bedford was owned by H. J. Phillips and Sons Ltd of Battersea and was photographed in Fernhurst on a lunch stop as part of its London-Midhurst Sanatorium service.

Below: HLY 480 (K180) of Birch Bros. This Leyland PD1 received a 52-seat lowbridge body built by the owner, being rebodied in 1956 by MCW. Originally a London bus operator, dating back to the 19th century, the Birch organisation also became involved in bus bodying on a large scale during the period surrounding World War 1 and operated a number of London motor bus services in the 1920s. However, these were absorbed by LPTB and Birch concentrated mainly on the London-Hitchin-Bedford-Rushden limited stop service which started in 1928.

Area Agreement Stronghold

With some of the earliest major provincial operators in the
South Eastern Traffic Area it followed that it was the scene of
early area agreements. Until World War 2 its nature was much
more residential than industrial and the developments which
both accompanied and followed that conflict included the
provision of earlier journeys. Postwar growth was remarkable
but it was the first area to lose traffic markedly to the private car
competition.

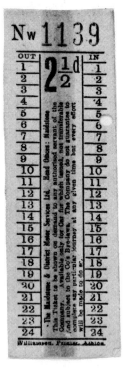

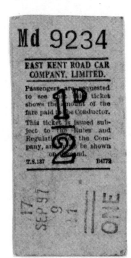

Left: East Kent suffered considerably during the war, becoming the 'Busman's Malta' since it was in the front line with occupied France a little over 20 miles away. The garage and offices at Dover were badly damaged and as a result the company acquired this office in Pencester Road, still in use today.

Below: Canterbury garage was also damaged during the war. This early postwar scene shows the bus park situated opposite these premises, with a cross section of the fleet at that period — Dennis Lancets, Leyland Titans and Guy Arabs.

Top: The original East Kent bus station in Canterbury was a rather cramped and primitive site at St Peter's, which was eventually replaced in 1956. AJG 6, a Park Royal-bodied Leyland Titan TD5 and new in 1938 stands next to two wartime Guy Arabs.

Above: Queues at Sandwich with JG8706, a Dennis Lancet, alongside a Leyland Cub on service 74, a local service to Ash and Westmarsh, the latter point now no longer being served by any public transport.

Right: East Kent was one of the few operators to purchase numbers of Morris Commercials, including these relatively short-lived Imperial double-deckers. JG 3230, new in 1933 and the last of its type to be delivered, is seen in Ashford on the joint service with Maidstone & District, between Folkestone and Maidstone. These vehicles had a fairly short life being proved not very successful.

Above: Faversham was the border town between two area agreement companies, Maidstone & District and East Kent. This photograph shows three Maidstone & District buses in the town. One of the Leyland Titans behind the Dennis 30cwt single-decker is showing Dartford which was served on a regular basis by M&D until the formation of London Transport when the local services west of Gravesend and a number of vehicles were transferred to that organisation.

Left: One of the 50 single-deck Guy trolleybuses purchased by Hastings Tramways to assist in the replacement of trams in 1928. In 1935 Maidstone & District purchased the system and the livery of the vehicles changed from maroon to green. Trolleybuses continued to be operated until 1959.

Below left: At Dungeness with the Romney, Hythe and Dymchurch Railway in the background; Carey Bros, which provided a New Romney-Lydd service, was one of the few independents in East Kent territory, as seen in this view with a Bedford WTB.

Above: LKP 42 one of four Dennis Falcons delivered to Maidstone & District with Dennis bodies, new in 1950, picking up passengers at Weald village on the infrequent service to Tonbridge previously operated by Ashline. London Transport inherited and provided the major service to the village which is still maintained by London Country.

Right: Maidstone & District acquired a number of vehicles from independent operators. This Commer Invader 6TK, KJ 1863 built in 1931, came from Medway Bus Owners. It was fitted with Chatham Motor Co bodywork and is standing in Sevenoaks bus station next to the West Kent Motor Services Dennis Ace.

Below right: Possibly one of the last purpose-built open-top double-deck vehicles in Great Britain, FKO 230 a Weymann-bodied Leyland Titan TD5 of Maidstone & District, stands at Battle. Seen on a wartime journey on a February Saturday the upper deck could well have been somewhat daunting.

Above: The picturesque village of Tenterden with two Leyland Titan TD4s of Maidstone & District.

Left: Some of the early examples of higher capacity single-deck vehicles were purchased by Maidstone & District. This Commer Contender, UKN 210, with two-stroke diesel engine and Harrington integral construction body, was one of 11 similar buses built in 1955. This photograph was taken when one-man-operation was being introduced by M&D on a number of routes from Tunbridge Wells.

Below left: Maidstone Corporation operated a small trolleybus network which had replaced most of the tram system. KO 8896 (18) was built by Ransomes, Sims & Jefferies with bodywork by the same manufacturer, delivered in 1928 as part of a fleet of eight similar vehicles which lasted until just after World War 2. The other seven prewar trolley buses were similar in outline but constructed by English Electric.

Above: Maidstone Corporation gradually increased its fleet of motor buses to serve growing housing development. AKO 390 (34) was one of 14 Crossley Condor VR6 buses acquired between 1934 and 1940.

Right: Newbury and District was part of the Red & White group by the time it was sold to the British Transport Commission and passed to Thames Valley in 1950. CRX 280, a Guy Arab II with Gardner 5LW engine, was a typical wartime utility vehicle.

Below: Because deliveries of new buses were restricted during the early years of World War 2, operators co-operated over the exchange of vehicles to help with demands for additional transport. East Kent loaned JG 8206, a Leyland Titan TD4, to Thames Valley where it acquired fleet number 110. Since public transport was vital to the community and many services were having difficulty in meeting demand, the Minister of War Transport issued an order in 1941 to make it an offence to buy or sell buses without his prior authority.

Left and below: One of only two Leyland Titans delivered to Aldershot & District, ECG 943 (L1) — a TD7 — was delivered early in the war as an 'unfrozen' vehicle. The East Lancs bodywork was mainly to prewar specification. Although mainly a Dennis operator, the Aldershot company turned to AECs in the 1950s as in this example of a new Reliance with a Strachans coach body. Such vehicles could be found on the Farnham-London express service as well as excursions and tours.

Right: Gosport and Fareham, originally a tram operator, was a subsidiary of the Provincial Tramways Group. Converting to buses in 1929, an interesting fleet was maintained, including on the left EHO 282 an AEC Regal, originating from Yelloway as a single-decker in 1932 and acquired from the War Department in 1942. A double-deck body was fitted by Reading the Portsmouth builder. The Park Royal-bodied Guy Arab, EHO 868, was rebuilt to open top in 1958 and lasted until 1969.

Below right: A further two Gosport and Fareham vehicles. JOT 288 was a 1951 Guy Arab III with Guy bodywork, while FHO 604 was one of a batch of four AEC Regent IIs with Reading bodies delivered in 1947.

Below: The independent Hants and Sussex developed into a sizeable undertaking operating various, mainly rural services in and around Southdown territory, before eventually finding itself compelled to relinquish many operations during the early 1950s. Here, DR 9064, a Dennis Lance previously with Plymouth Corporation, was photographed on the Graffham-Midhurst service.

Left: Thomas Tilling entered into provincial bus operation after 1914, having concluded an agreement with LGOC which restricted expansion in the capital. Local services in Brighton were developed and in November 1935 a separate company, Brighton Hove and District, was set up to administer this network. AEC Regents and then Bristols, were the mainstay of the fleet. This rear view of a K5G shows the very informative side and rear destination blinds employed at the time. (Below) As part of the co-ordination of operations with Brighton Corporation, agreed in 1937, BH&D also operated a small fleet of trolleybuses as seen in this view of CPM 101 (6344), an AEC 661T with Weymann H54R bodywork.

Above: Pool Valley bus station was the main terminal for Southdown bus services in Brighton. This prewar photograph shows a variety of Leylands and the more elderly Tilling-Stevens vehicles of the company.

Below: Two of the three-axle Leyland Tiger TS6T vehicles with centre entrance Short bodies and 8.6litre engines purchased especially for the Eastbourne-Beachy Head service where this photograph was taken.

Right: Southdown was allocated Guy Arabs during the war as represented by this 1944 Northern Counties-bodied vehicle.

Below right: Tramocar operated along Worthing seafront using Shelvoke and Drewry vehicles (one seen at rear of picture) although taken over in 1938 by Southdown. The following year, the new owner purchased two Harrington-bodied Dennis Falcons to operate on the service, retaining the name for goodwill purposes.

Left: Southdown marked the postwar traffic increase by instituting a considerable mileage of new routes. Among these was the 19 emanating from Lewes and subsequently attaining Newick. This Leyland Tiger Cub is seen at the Rainbow Inn north of Cooksbridge.

Below: Crossley vehicles were relatively few and far between in the south, but apart from Maidstone, seen earlier, Portsmouth Corporation also favoured the make. EBK 24 is a DD42/5T model, with a locally-built 52-seat Reading body, built in 1948. Behind is one of Portsmouth's Leyland Titan PD1s.

Right: Portsmouth again and almost the end of this chapter; facing the camera is STP 996, a Metro-Cammell bodied Leyland Titan PD3, while DTP 811, a Leyland PD1A with a Reading body, heads in the opposite direction.

Below right: Further along the coast, Southampton standardised, postwar, on Guy Arab vehicles and Park Royal-bodied FOW 455 typifies the scene in the 1950s.

Above: Earlier Southampton purchased Leylands, partly for tram replacement as this 1939 Leyland Titan TD5 with a Park Royal body shows. It lasted until 1951.

Below: Wilts and Dorset Motor Services, centred on Salisbury, developed a comprehensive network, eventually embracing Basingstoke, Andover and Amesbury. It was also known for renovating vehicles and CHR 493, a lowbridge Bristol K5G, new 'unfrozen' in 1940, was rebuilt by its owner in 1953.

In National's Southern Territory

After the cessation of its steambus operations in Central London the National Omnibus & Transport Co Ltd devoted itself to expansion of its provincial interests in the West Country, the South Midlands and Essex. After the railways received official consent for road operations the west was divided appropriately between Western and Southern National. Operations have always tended to be of moderate intensity and independent operators have remained numerous.

Right: The origins of the Royal Blue express services owned by Elliott Bros went back to the 19th century, and later with motor vehicles were to develop long distance services to and from Bournemouth. In 1935 the business was sold to Thomas Tilling with the express operations passing to Western and Southern National and the tours and private hire to Hants and Dorset. This early AEC Regal, LJ 1516, is in fact on an early Omnibus Society tour which included a visit to Stonehenge for sunrise on Midsummer's Day where the photograph was taken.

Below right: Postwar, the Royal Blue fleet was typified by vehicles such as this Bristol L6B with coachwork by Beadle. It was delivered in 1948 and lasted well, until 1969.

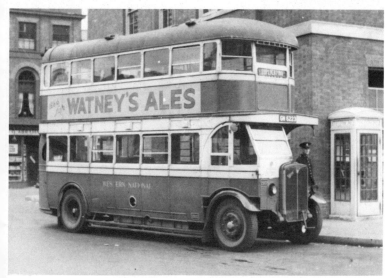

Above left: Western and Southern National also acquired Bedford OWBs during the war. This delightful scene shows DOD 560 (511), new in 1943, at Crackington Haven having traversed the water splash on the Camelford-Bude service. Note the offside bonnet cover removed to improve engine cooling along the hilly route.

Below left: Over in Taunton, standing at the Parade, is this elderly-looking ex-Thomas Tilling and Brighton, Hove and District AEC Regent with a Dodson body. GN 6223 was acquired by Western National in 1945, received fleet number 2902 and was withdrawn four years later to become a breakdown tender.

Below: An interesting line-up at the Truro garage of Western National with two Bedford OBs, coach HUO 697 (544) new in 1947 and Beadle bus-bodied HUO 672 (514), originally delivered to Southern National, but transferred to the Western fleet in 1955. In the centre is DR 8715 a vintage Leyland Titan TD1, but fitted with a Gardner 6LW engine. The vehicle had been rebodied by Beadle in 1942.

Above left: A much earlier scene at
Truro with MW 4154 (2843), a
Leyland Lion PLSC3 new to Western
National in February 1929 and
rebodied by Mumford in 1936. In the
background is a Dennis Mace.

Left: Now coming a little more up-to-
date and seen when virtually new, this
45-seat Bristol LS5G of Western
National arrived in 1953 and helped
modernise the fleet.

Above: Devon General, a BET
subsidiary after its takeover of the
National Electric Construction
interest, operated within a fairly
compact area in South Devon, with a
co-ordination agreement with Exeter
Corporation. These Leyland Lion
LT7s with Harrington bodywork and
wartime livery stand at Exeter Central
station.

Above right: The graceful lines of
Duple bodywork can be seen here in
this view of Grey Cars LTA 633, a
1950 AEC Regal, one of 12 acquired
that year. Others of the class can be
seen behind. Grey Cars was the
coaching unit of Devon General after
purchase of the Torquay interests of
Timpsons.

Right: An all-Leyland Titan TD5 of
Exeter Corporation, EFJ 161 was
purchased in 1938 and in 1957 passed
to Birch Bros of London. Note the use
of route letters rather than numbers on
the Exeter network.

Above: A Ford van and a Morris Commercial of F. T. Marshall providing a service between Torrington station and any part of the town. Torrington was the railhead for a large area of North Devon until in 1925, quite late for railway development, the North Devon and Cornwall Railway was opened to Halwill Junction.

Right: Safeway Services of South Petherton has provided stage services into Yeovil for many years. The ever popular Bedford OB was no exception to this fleet as seen by GYC 330.

Below: On the quay at Bridgwater this Bedford OWB, FYD 306 delivered in 1943 to Haybittel of Otterhampton, collects another passenger for Stolford.

Above: Another postwar loan, this time an AEC Regal from Tillings of London on hire to the Bristol company and seen in Marlborough.

Below: Tilling STs went from London to a number of operators. When new in 1932, GP 6241 was sent to Brighton but was photographed in Bath on loan to Bristol Tramways during the war years.

Top: Tilling Stevens B39A7, OD 7780, with Eastern Counties bodywork stands at Bideford before preparing to work a local service for Southern National.

Above: The West Country scene ends on a holiday note. This view of the premises of Swanage Coaches and the popular Duple Vega bodywork produced in large numbers during the middle and late 1950s.

Amongst the Valleys

Left: No 200 in the Western Welsh fleet was this oil-engined Leyland Tiger TS8 seen standing beside a Guy Arab II of Red & White (755: EWO 755) with Duple austerity double-deck bodywork.

Western Welsh developed into being the largest operating company in South Wales with services covering the area from Aberystwyth through most parts of the industrial south to the agricultural areas of Monmouthshire. Just before World War 2 some 400 vehicles were owned. A mixture of services was maintained from meeting the relatively straightforward needs of rural population, with moderate frequencies augmented on market days, to intensive urban operations coping with continuous shift working, especially at the numerous colleries. Problems existed in mixing miners with other passengers, partly overcome by increasing the number of pithead baths and restricting colliery workers on the ordinary services.

Left: An all-Leyland Lion LT3 of Western Welsh with an illuminable sign on its roof. These were applied to single-deckers for some time.

Below left: Pictured in June 1940 is this Caerphilly UDC oil-engined Dennis Lancet, CTX 948, with bodywork by the same manufacturer. Introduced in 1938, it had a relatively short life, being withdrawn in 1944. A Western Welsh Tiger stands opposite.

Above: Rhondda Tramways favoured AECs as TG 2466, a 1931 Regal with 30-seat Weymann bodywork (later upseated to 32), shows. Three years afterwards the last trams were operated by this undertaking and the name was changed to the more appropriate Rhonnda Transport Company. In the background is a Rhonnda Bristol D type.

Below: The West Monmouthshire Omnibus Board, owned by two urban district councils, took over services from a number of independents. This picture shows the famous Bargoed Hill route between Bargoed and Markham. Special vehicles were needed for this operation including at first some Saurers. Charles Klapper took this photograph just after the outbreak of war in 1939, showing a Weymann-bodied Leyland Bull TSC9 built in 1935 descending the 1 in $4\frac{1}{4}$ hill. Just after the picture was taken, the photographer nearly spent a night in Newport police station. The last train had gone before he could explain his innocence in only taking transport photographs and not spying for a foreign power!

Above: A line up of mainly wartime deliveries to Pontypridd UDC. On the right of the picture ETG 138, a Bristol K5G, was delivered in 1939 while further to the left is No 39, a Bristol K6A which arrived in 1944. Sandwiched in between these vehicles and another Bristol are Guy Arab IIs.

Below: This earlier view of a Pontypridd vehicle shows a 1931 Bristol B type, TG 1146, with Eastwood and Kenning body designed for one-man operation, but not used for such. It was one of the vehicles bought for tram replacement.

Above right: Merthyr Tydfil owned this postwar Bristol K6G with Davies 56-seat body, delivered in 1948.

Right: The Bristol Lodekka became one of the standard vehicles of the Tilling organisation which also absorbed the Red & White Group in 1948, centred on Chepstow, TAX 237, a LD6G, is typical of this type.

Above: ATH 327, an Albion Valkyrie of West Wales Motors Ltd, based at Tycroes near Ammanford, represents the many independents in the west of the principality.

Right: South Wales Transport, a BET subsidiary, was connected with tramway undertakings in Swansea and this 1938 lowbridge Leyland Titan TD5, bodied by Weymann, was in fact owned by the associated Swansea Improvements and Tramways Company, to take over from tram operation.

Below: Almost in Wales, BU 8262, a Leyland TD3 with Roe bodywork and new to Oldham Corporation, is seen on hire to Red & White in Chepstow during the war years.

Independent Enterprise

On and around the border between England and Wales there flourishes a number of independent operators providing valuable services between the scattered and remote settlements and the various market towns.

Yeomans of Canon Pyon was one of the largest independents in this area whose origins extend back to 1920 but had by the early 1940s developed many daily services in a triangle formed, at its points, by Hereford, Craven Arms and Knighton. It was an operator with which friendly relationships were maintained by the larger undertakings. A deal was struck with Midland Red in December 1934 when a number of Midland Red rural services in the Hereford and Leominster area were acquired in return for offering that concern fare protection within Hereford City.

An agreement also existed for through bookings from Yeoman's Hereford-Kington-New Radnor service to the Crosville route from Kington to Llandrindod Wells. Wartime increases in traffic brought about a need for double-deckers since previously mainly single-deck AEC Regals were operated, together with Crossleys, a Thornycroft and a Surrey Dodge.

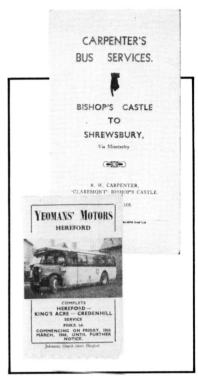

Left: This AEC Regal of Yeomans, VJ 3281, was new in 1930 but rebuilt in 1944 when the seating in the Smith body was increased by two to 34.

Left: At Hereford, the most interesting vehicle in this picture is perhaps HF 9399, a 1934 AEC Q, new to Wallasey in 1934 and acquired by Yeomans in 1946.

Below left: Once more at Hereford bus station, DCJ 299 of Yeomans is a 1945 Daimler CWA6 with Duple utility bodywork. It stands beside OG 380, an AEC Regent built in 1930 and acquired in 1946 from Birmingham Corporation.

Above: Salopia was another of the more important independents and is represented by UJ 7432 — a Leyland LZ2 with Santus bodywork which lasted from 1936 to 1951. Behind it stands a Tilling-Stevens Express of Worthen and District and previously West Yorkshire Road Car.

Below: Mid Wales Motorways Ltd was registered in 1937, uniting a number of local operators providing services in the Newtown, Montgomery and Welshpool areas. As elsewhere in this region, to reach many of the communities, tortuous roads had to be traversed. EP 6595, a Dodge coach, is seen with a typical cross-section of the local community.

Above left: This Bedford WTB belonged to the Ludlow Motor Company which traded as Clun Valley Motor Services.

Below left: A Commer (WP 6594) of T. A. Owen is about to leave Knighton for Llanfair Waterdine. This operator also provided a market day service through to Newton via Felindre over the Kerry Hills, famous for a breed of sheep.

Below: This Bedford OWB of Tippings is seen here in Ledbury on the service to Putley.

Above right: The conductor assists passengers using this Bedford OWB of Mr R. Carpenter of Bishops Castle, Shropshire whose network of market day services operated to such places as Newtown as well as others which brought traffic to the operator's home town. A more regular service was also operated to Shrewsbury, co-ordinatated with Midland Red.

Right: Hailstone of Churchstoke, owned a number of small vehicles in order to negotiate even more difficult thoroughfares. UJ 9058 was one such Bedford seen loading in Shrewsbury.

Preparing the Harvest

One of the few classic books about the bus industry was Crosland Taylor's *The Sowing and the Harvest* which described the development of the Crosville company from a car manufacturer into a substantial bus operator. After its reshaping in 1930 it had some 2,000 route miles and 650 vehicles whilst its merger with Western Transport from 1 May 1933 brought its route mileage to some 2,500 and its fleet to 800. Much of the Crosville territory is sparsely populated and its best harvests came fairly early in the postwar period before the private car had made its inroads particularly into offpeak and market day traffic.

Below: In North Wales, this prewar view shows a Crosville Leyland Cub pausing while working the Beddgelert and Penygwryd service.

Above: Photographed while reversing at Crewe station, this wartime Northern Counties Guy Arab I, FFM 218, was built in 1942 and lasted until 1954.

Left: The popular light country bus introduced during the late 1950s in the Tilling Group was the Bristol SC4LK with ECW bodywork. This Crosville example, 789 EFM, was equipped for one-man operation, and is seen on the Penybontfawr to Oswestry service.

Right: EY 2741 was one of six Bristol O type, of the Royal Blue fleet of the Llandudno Coaching and Carriage Co Ltd which began stage carriage operations with motor buses in 1921 and had by December 1929 83 buses and 11 coaches. The LMS Railway had bought an interest that month and five months later the company was absorbed in the reconstituted Crosville company.

Below right: This elderly Daimler, photographed around 1938, had been acquired in 1926 by W. S. Jones of Beddgelert to run bus services into Caernarvon. However, the chassis, fitted with a Strachan and Brown 24-seat body in that year, dated back to pre-1914 days.

Below: A 1938 view of a Morris-Commercial, UN 6581, of Wrights, operating between Chirk and Glynceiriog. The route was formerly covered by the 2ft 4½in gauge Glyn Valley Railway which had suspended operations in 1933, due to the impact of road competition. The passenger in this view, according to Charles, had just begged some petrol for a cigarette lighter!

Serving the Black Country (and District) the Friendly Way

The friendly Midland Red company, as it liked to be known, served most parts of central England from Nottingham and Northampton in the east to Shrewsbury and Hereford in the west. Some 2,000 vehicles were owned, mostly of its own construction, presenting an almost unique scene in Great Britain.

Below: A Hereford City service in 1934 is worked by a 1928 SOS QL with Brush body . The last two vehicles of this type were not withdrawn until 1950.

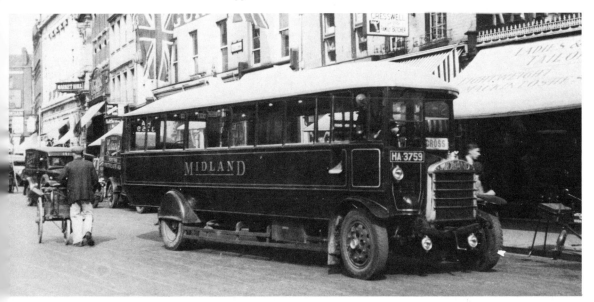

Above: A 1930 SOS RR at Leicester (Southgate Street) garage. The bodies and registrations of this class were originally fitted to 1929 SOS XL chassis, but in 1930, the bodies were transferred to the much improved RR chassis. The destination of the vehicles is interesting as this service was exchanged in February 1932 with Barton Transport for a Birmingham to Nottingham service which became Midland Red's X99 route. Vehicles of the RR class were transferred on extended loan to the Potteries Motor Traction Company in 1940, to meet urgent transport requirements of ordnance factories at Swynnerton and Radway Green. Most did not return to Midland Red, being withdrawn and scrapped by PMT. Potteries had for many years operated SOS single and double-deckers.

Above right: A 1930 SOS IM4 from Shrewsbury after duplicating a service journey as far as Church Stretton. The dark roof, white flashes and masked lights show that the photograph was taken during the early years of World War 2.

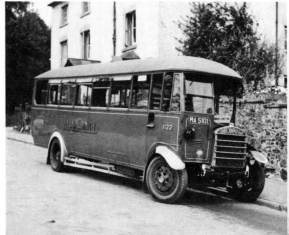

Right: An almost new 1938 SOS FEDD near Dudley garage. The Dudley to Stourbridge route was converted to bus operation in 1930 when the Dudley, Stourbridge & District electric tram service ceased. The tram depot at Brierley Hill (Harts Hill) was converted to a bus garage and purpose-built garages were opened at Dudley and Stourbridge. Harts Hill provided most of the vehicles for the service, but Dudley and Stourbridge also had a small allocation. Locally the service was always referred to as the D and S. The route and all three garages passed to the West Midland PTE in 1973.

Above: A 1944 Guy Arab II with Weymann body, soon after delivery, stands outside the Odeon Cinema in New Street, Birmingham. This bus is one of a large number of Guy double-decks allocated to Sutton (Coldfield) garage at that time. All were fitted with five-cylinder Gardner engines and were extensively rebuilt during 1950/51. Withdrawal had been completed by 1957.

Left: Although most wartime Guy Arabs were allocated to Sutton (Coldfield) garage (the 20 postwar Arab IIIs were at Dudley), a small number was operated from Leicester (Sandacre Street) garage. This early postwar picture shows passengers boarding an evening departure.

Above: With the successful operation of the wartime prototype vehicles, following D. M. Sinclair's experience with the SE4 and SE6 high-capacity single-deckers of Northern General, 100 BMMO S6 single-deckers were delivered in 1946 and 1947. Bodies were by Brush and Metro-Cammell. Initially all garages were allocated at least one example in order to gain driving and operational experience. A demonstration chassis visited each garage prior to its receiving a complete bus. The picture shows the one originally allocated to Evesham with bodywork by Brush. With the delivery of later buses built to the newer increased width, the S6s were mainly concentrated at more rural garages. All were lengthened by Roe in 1953. Withdrawals started in 1961 and were completed by 1965.

Right: The forerunner of the postwar series of double-decked vehicles stands near the rear entrance to Bearwood garage. Introduced in 1945 and fitted with a Weymann all-metal four-bay body to Midland Red designs, it was to a national influence on double-deck styling. Classified D1, it had an 8litre BMMO engine. In 1949 platform doors were fitted to test their feasibility for services with frequent stops. It was withdrawn in 1961.

Above: Interior of the enquiry office at the rebuilt bus station and garage in Stourbridge. The new complex replaced the garage, open forecourt and wooden passenger shelter and enquiry office erected in 1929. Rebuilding work was completed in 1958 and passed to the West Midland PTE in 1973.

Below: Stratford Blue was a small efficient operator of just over 40 vehicles, being a subsidiary of the Midland Red company from 1935 when it bought the shares from Midland Counties Electric Supply, although SB operated few vehicles built by its owner. GUE 245, an all-Leyland Titan PD2/1, was immaculately kept, like all buses in the fleet.

Above: A little to the south, and a lot earlier, this Gilford 1660T, UL 9488, with Wycombe 22-seat body, was new to the Great Western Railway, but passed to the Bristol company in 1932 as part of an agreement whereby the directly-controlled bus services of the railway went to associated road operators. This vehicle was based at Cheltenham and maintained the service to Oxford, co-ordinated with the trains for which it had been purchased.

Left: City of Oxford Motor Services introduced this Weymann-bodied AEC Regent in 1940. The operator had a distinctive livery of red with maroon tops and window frames plus duck egg green waist rails, and centred on the university city provided both local services as well as interurban operations to neighbouring towns.

Above right: Another Weymann body, but this time on an oil-engined AEC Regal with fleet number one, built in 1937 and withdrawn in 1952. It is seen in Chipping Norton.

Right: Whittles of Highley established both a network of local services to such places as Kidderminster and Bridgnorth as well as a successful coaching business. Surrounded by private cars of the early 1950s, then posing little threat to the bus industry, is KAW 677, a Leyland Royal Tiger PSU1/17 with Leyland bodywork which was operated by Whittles between 1954 and 1960.

Above right: Within the Black Country, Wolverhampton was an important trolleybus operator. Much development work took place there and during the 1920s bus building techniques were employed for trolleybuses rather than using those heavier designs based on tram technology. Guy trolleybuses dominated the Wolverhampton fleet in the earlier years, as repesented by UK 9971 (71) introduced in 1931. Nearer the camera is JW 993, a Sunbeam MS2, introduced in 1932, and on the left, UK 9640 is a rare vehicle indeed, an AJS Commodore with body by the same manufacturer. This was originally a demonstrator built in 1930. It lasted until 1937.

Right: Walsall Corporation was a large scale Dennis operator in prewar days. This fairly late petrol-engined Ace model, constructed in 1937 and fitted with Park Royal body, stayed with the operator until 1952.

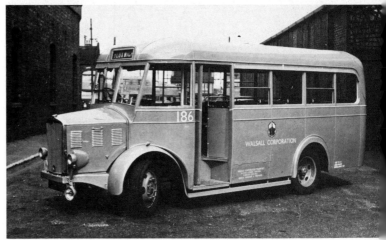

Below: Working on a Leicester-Loughborough service is this Maudslay SF40, belonging to H. Boyer of Rothley. The SF40 was an early attempt to achieve maximum capacity on a single-deck chassis within the then applicable dimensions.

Above: Barton Transport, one of the major independents, was a pioneer in the use of alternative fuels, with coal gas in two world wars, and with diesel fuel in the early 1930s. Among the vehicles demonstrated in 1931 was the modified Gilford.

Below: A smart-looking Derby Corporation Guy BTX trolleybus with Brush bodywork, constructed in 1934, to provide for tram replacement, which took place between 1932 and 1935.

Above: At nearby Nottingham, this Corporation AEC Regent was built in 1936 and was photographed in wartime with a West Bridgford AEC Regent on the far right. Trams were abandoned in 1936 although the track is clearly visible.

Below: AEC Regals with Lawton bodywork of Browns Motor Co (Tunstall) Ltd in the autumn of 1932. The company had been formed eight years previously to take over a family business and from the time these Regals were delivered it bought mostly AECs until the advent of a dozen Bedford OWBs in wartime.

The Eastern Flank

To its south, this is part of the National territory, served by Eastern National and to the north, two operators which took over areas pioneered by United Automobile. Throughout, various independent undertakings prospered, some of whom have now disappeared while others still battle on.

Seen at Brentwood, perhaps best described as one of the 'gateways' to the east. The City Coach Company acquired from Brentwood and District in 1936 this Surrey Dodge, BNO 395 with 20-seat Duple bodywork. On the right is DXM 833, a Bedford WTB again with Duple bodywork which was new to Orange Luxury Coaches in 1937, but acquired by City in 1940. The City organisation had substantial bus interests in London during the 1920s, but was obliged to sell these to London Transport in 1934. Thereafter City concentrated on a Southend-Wood Green service but acquired also some local bus interests in Brentwood and Laindon. The company later sold out to the British Transport Commission and the operations are now part of the Eastern National empire.

Above: Westcliff-on-Sea Motor Services, whose stage and excursion operations were based on Southend and South Essex, at one time was also involved on the Wood Green operation. It was absorbed by Eastern National as part of the process by the BTC to reorganise its various bus interests into logical and geographically simpler operating units. EJN 633 (344) was a 39-seat Bristol LWL5G which carried the Westcliff name for a while under Eastern National ownership.

Below: Hicks Brothers, based in the Braintree and Bishops Stortford areas with its blue and yellow Guys and Leylands, was also taken under the Eastern National wing. WH 1554, new to Bolton Corporation in 1929, was a Leyland Titan TD1 acquired by Hicks in 1936. The rear of WH 4908, also a Leyland Titan, can be seen. This too came from Bolton but during the war had been lent first to London Transport and later to Midland Red.

WESTCLIFF ON SEA
MOTOR SERVICES LIMITED

Official Time Tables
JULY 21st, 1948
and until further notice
SOUTHEND ON SEA
Price : Fourpence

FOR UP-TO-DATE ROUTE MAP SEE CENTRE PAGES
WESTCLIFF ON-SEA
MOTOR SERVICES LTD
OFFICIAL TIME TABLE
OCT. 1930.   OCT. 1930.

THORPE BAY LAUNDRY CO., LTD

DRYING BY SEA BREEZES.

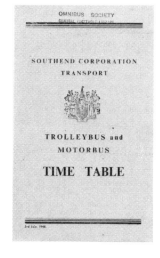

OMNIBUS SOCIETY

SOUTHEND CORPORATION
TRANSPORT

TROLLEYBUS and
MOTORBUS
TIME TABLE

ENTERPRISE
(SCUNTHORPE)
PASSENGER
SERVICES LTD.
TIME TABLE

MAY, 1948
Registered Office :
Bus Station, Scunthorpe.
A. Drury, Managing Director.
PRICE 4 PENCE

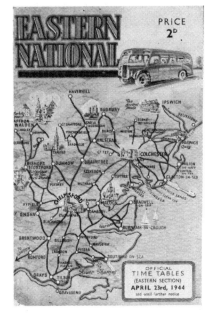

EASTERN NATIONAL
PRICE 2D

OFFICIAL
TIME TABLES
(EASTERN SECTION)
APRIL 23rd, 1944
and until further notice

EASTERN NATIONAL
Official Time Table
PRICE 1D
SUMMER SERVICES

MIDLAND SECTION
JULY 1st to SEPT. 30th, 1932.

NORFOLK AREA
NORWICH

EASTERN COUNTIES
OMNIBUS · COMPANY · LIMITED

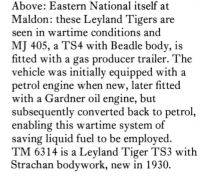

Above: Eastern National itself at Maldon: these Leyland Tigers are seen in wartime conditions and MJ 405, a TS4 with Beadle body, is fitted with a gas producer trailer. The vehicle was initially equipped with a petrol engine when new, later fitted with a Gardner oil engine, but subsequently converted back to petrol, enabling this wartime system of saving liquid fuel to be employed. TM 6314 is a Leyland Tiger TS3 with Strachan bodywork, new in 1930.

Left: Acquired from Brighton, Hove and District in 1952, NJ 9057 is a Bristol G05G and was pictured at Kirby-Le-Soken, bound for Walton and Frinton.

Below left: Motorbus operation in Southend is represented by this AEC Regent with English Electric lowbridge body, delivered in 1937 and withdrawn 21 years later. The vehicle went on loan to Coventry during part of the war period.

Above right: Southend-on-Sea operated a small network of trolleybuses to help in tram replacement, as seen in these pictures of JN 2817 (162) — an English Electric-bodied AEC 661T which lasted until 1950; and (right) Garrett HJ 7363 standing among some withdrawn trams. Trams disappeared finally in 1942 while trolleybuses lasted until the early 1950s when a co-ordination agreement was finally concluded with Eastern National.

Right: Eastern Counties operating territory covered an extensive part of East Anglia, having been formed in 1931 by amalgamation of a number of well established undertakings, including part of the operations of United Automobile. Included in these acquisitions was the bodybuilding plant of United at Lowestoft, which later as Eastern Coach Works, has continued to maintain a dominant position in the British bus building industry. In this picture, an Associated Daimler 423, VF 2826 with an Eastern Counties body, is standing at Cambridge on a local service. The vehicle was one of those loaned to London Transport during the war years.

Below: Southwold was served until 1929 by a delightful narrow gauge railway which terminated near the Eastern Counties garage where BVF 112, a Bristol JO5G, was photographed. Delivered in 1937, it was one of the vehicles fitted with perimeter seating during the war to increase carrying capacity. The rear of LNG 293, a Bristol KS5G can be seen.

Above left: Premier Travel is one of the many independent operators still running in East Anglia. Based on Cambridge, its network of local bus services and later express operations extended far and wide. This magnificent Daimler CVD6 fitted with Wilks and Meade 33-seat body was delivered new to Premier Travel in 1948 and lasted until 1960.

Below left: Standing in front of this Duple-bodied Bedford OB are Mrs Lainson, Arthur Lainson (second from right), one of the founders of Premier Travel and later a president of the Omnibus Society, and Mr W. F. Matthews, director of the company. The vehicle was delivered to Premier Travel in 1945 and was painted in a chocolate and maroon livery while the normal colour scheme was, being a Cambridge based operator, a light blue.

Below: Cambridge in wartime with Premier Travel: HX 3464, a Gilford AS6 with Duple bodywork, carried fleet number one, and was new to Crouch End Luxury Coaches. It was finally withdrawn in 1948. It appears the American servicemen have made a favourable impression upon some young ladies of the university town!

Above: Another independent, but to the east at Halesworth, was Naylors. Its ex-Don Everall Bedford OWB, but this time with Mulliner bodywork, helped work a number of local services to neighbouring towns such as Ipswich and Lowestoft. Delivered in 1946, this particular bus remained with the operator for nine years.

Below: A local authority bus business which is no more, having been absorbed by Eastern Counties, Lowestoft Corporation is represented by FBJ 374, a Massey-bodied Guy Arab II, one of six delivered in 1945. Originally a tram undertaking, Lowestoft converted to buses in 1931.

Above right: The Lincolnshire Road Car Company, created in 1928, was a part of the Tilling/British Automobile Traction group and acquired a number of independent undertakings, as well as part of the United Automobile's empire covering Lincolnshire. Since the company passed to the Tilling group in 1942, and to BTC in 1948, Bristol vehicles became standard during the 1950s. This early postwar highbridge Bristol K stands at Kings Lynn bound for Spalding with a more elderly Leyland behind.

One of the important acquisitions by Lincolnshire was Enterprise (Scunthorpe) Passenger Services Ltd, which sold out to BTC in 1950. Enterprise was a large undertaking by independent standards with over 150 vehicles at the time of takeover. It had a long history, being known at one time by the name of Enterprise and Silver Dawn. Bedford OWB, CFU 322 built in 1943, is seen (below) on the Scunthorpe to Althorpe service; while AEC Regent DBE 970, delivered in 1946 with Burlingham lowbridge bodywork, is working the route from Scunthorpe to New Holland (right) where connections were made with the ferry for Hull.

Above: The Provincial Tramways Company developed tramways in a number of areas, including Gosport where the name lives on, and both Grimsby and Cleethorpes. The two local authorities acquired the operating interests of Provincial in their respective areas and thereafter that name disappeared from this part of the country. However, during the company's existence motor buses were acquired, including some three-axled Chevrolets as seen with FW 119.

Left: AMB 834 was a Foden DDG6 demonstrator with Burlingham body which was found in the fleet of Ebor, an independent operating in the Mansfield area, the business of which was acquired by Mansfield District in 1950.

Dark Satanic Mills

This selection covers some of the interesting concerns from the Humber to the Scottish border; for example both area agreement operators and some large independent operators, a number of which were acquired by the British Transport Commission, which was anxious to build up its interests in the passenger transport business.

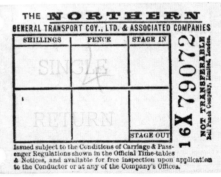

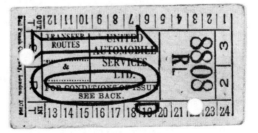

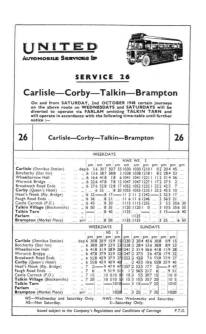

UNITED
AUTOMOBILE SERVICES LTD

SERVICE 26

Carlisle—Corby—Talkin—Brampton

On and from SATURDAY, 2nd OCTOBER 1948 certain journeys on the above route on WEDNESDAYS and SATURDAYS will be diverted to operate via FARLAM omitting TALKIN TARN and will operate in accordance with the following time-table until further notice :—

26	Carlisle—Corby—Talkin—Brampton		26

WEEKDAYS

		am	am	am	am	NWS	WS	S	pm	pm	pm
Carlisle (Omnibus Station)	dep	6	5 6	30 7	50 7	55	1030	1030	1210	1 02	2 04	45
Botcherby (Star Inn)	,, 6	13	6 38	7 58	8 3	1038	1038	1218	1 8	2 28	4 53
Wheelbarrow Hall	,, 6 16	6 41	8 1	8 6	1041	1041	1221	1 11	2 31	4 56
Warwick Bridge	,, 6 22	6 47	8 7	8 12	1047	1047	1227	1 17	2 37	5 2
Broadwath Road Ends	,, 6 27	6 52	8 12	8 17	1052	1052	1232	1 22	2 42	4 5 7
Corby (Queen's Hotel)	,, 6 55		8 20	1055	1055	1235	1 25	2 45	5 10
Head's Nook (Rly. Bridge)	,, 6 32		8 17	1 21	1 21	242		2 52	5 17
Faugh Road Ends	,, 6 36		8 21	11 6	11 6	246		2 56	5 21
Castle Carrack (P.O.)	,, 6 45		8 30	1115	1115	255		3 5	5 30	6 30
Talkin Village (Blacksmiths)	,, 6 50		8 35	1120	1120	1 0		3 10	5 35	6 35
Talkin Tarn			8 40	1125				3 15		6 40
Farlam					1125				
Brampton (Market Place)	arr		8 50	1135	1135		3 25		6 50

WEEKDAYS						SUNDAYS					
		pm	pm	pm	pm	NS	S	pm	pm	pm	
Carlisle (Omnibus Station)	dep	6 30	8 20	9 15	9 15	1230	2 20	4 56	6 30	8 09	15
Botcherby (Star Inn)	,, 6 38	8 28	9 23	9 23	1238	2 28	4 5 36	8 38	8 23
Wheelbarrow Hall	,, 6 41	8 31	9 28	9 28	1241	2 31	4 56	6 41	8 11	9 28
Warwick Bridge	,, 6 47	8 37	9 32	9 32	1247	2 37	5 2	6 47	8 17	9 32
Broadwath Road Ends	,, 6 52	8 42	9 37	9 37	1252	2 42	5 7	6 52	7 6	7 8	9 37
Corby (Queen's Hotel)	,, 6 55	8 45	9 40	9 40	,, 2 45	5 10	6 55	8 25	9 40
Head's Nook (Rly. Bridge)	,, 7 2		9 47	9 47	1257	2 52	5 17	7 2		9 47
Faugh Road Ends	,, 7 6		9 51	9 51	1 1	2 56	5 21	7 6		9 51
Castle Carrack (P.O.)	,, 7 15		10 0	10 0	10 3	5 05	5 30	7 15		10 0
Talkin Village (Blacksmiths)	,, 7 20		10 5	10 5	1 15	3 10	5 35	7 20		10 5
Talkin Tarn			1010		1 19	3 15		7 25		1010
Farlam									
Brampton (Market Place)	arr		1020			3 25	7 35		1020

WS—Wednesday and Saturday Only.   NWS—Not Wednesday and Saturday.
NS—Not Saturday.   S—Saturday Only.

Issued subject to the Company's Regulations and Conditions of Carriage   P.T.O.

UNITED

NORTHUMBERLAND DISTRICT
TIME TABLE
COMPLIMENTARY

1st JULY, 1934
Until Further Notice

PRICE TWOPENCE

OTHER DISTRICTS which UNITED SERVE :—
DURHAM, CLEVELAND, RIPON & SCARBOROUGH

Left: Kingston-upon-Hull Corporation had concluded co-ordination agreements with the neighbouring area agreement company, East Yorkshire Motor Services. This aided the conversion of trams to motorbus operation although trolleybuses were chosen as the main means of replacing railed transport. This started in 1937 and CRH 946, a Leyland model, is seen at the northern terminus of service 62 which took over from tram route S that year.

Below: East Yorkshire Roe-bodied Guy Arab GRH 199, built in 1944, included the Beverley Bar shape of the roof, necessary to negotiate, at that time, the shape of that structure. This was one of the few variations permitted to such utility vehicles.

Right: The neat lines of Eastern Coach Works design are shown in this postwar East Yorkshire vehicle, a Leyland Tiger PS1 delivered in 1948 and lasting in its owner's service until 1960.

Below right: Over on the coast at Bridlington, the White Bus Company provided local bus services using a variety of vehicles including this Leyland Titan TD2, UG 1052, fitted with Roe bodywork, new to Leeds Corporation. This vehicle was withdrawn by White Bus in 1950 and the operator was absorbed by East Yorkshire in 1955.

Below: The West Riding Automobile Company was one of the largest independent operators, whose origins were based on tramway operation from Wakefield and Pontefract, but by the early 1930s had converted to motorbus operation entirely. Acquisition by the British Transport Commission was thwarted and in 1950 a merger took place with J. Bullock & Son which helped create a substantial fleet of some 150 vehicles. Here, both of West Riding standing in Selby, are BHL 863, a Leyland Titan PD2/1 with Leyland bodywork, and behind, AHL 106, a Roe-bodied Guy Arab. Since the merger, West Riding has sold out and is now part of the National Bus Company.

Left: West Yorkshire developed two agreements whereby the company operated services on behalf of municipal undertakings. The York agreement was operative from 1934 and some vehicles were transferred to a separate fleet for this task. WW 7101 was one such bus. This all-Leyland Titan TD1 was delivered to West Yorkshire in 1928 but in 1935 went to York-West Yorkshire for replacement purposes.

Below left: Much of West Yorkshire territory was through fairly rural territory and in one case via Braithwaite farmhouse, near Keighley, as pictured here with BWT 755 a Bristol J05G of 1937 vintage. The service was subsequently adjusted so as to avoid this particular part of the route.

Below: Single-deck trolleybuses were never common in Great Britain but both Rotherham Corporation and adjoining Mexborough and Swinton Traction Company systems had examples. FET 347, an East Lancs-bodied Daimler CT6, was photographed at the Queens Head terminus at Maltby in May 1954 on the last day of operation of this particular service. Daimler trolleybuses were not common and some of those delivered to Rotherham were rebodied later as double-deckers.

Left: United Automobile purchased this Bristol J05G with Eastern Coach Works body in 1937, and in 1952 it passed to Durham District Services, to set up that undertaking and replace some of the vehicles acquired from the independents.

Below: XHN 402 was one of five Bristol LS6B Eastern Coach Works dual-purpose vehicles purchased by United Automobile in 1955. Here it is seen when new on the North Yorks Moor on service 58 from Scarborough to Whitby and Middlesbrough.

Right: Northern General was one of the few operators to purchase vehicles built by Midland Red. CN 4750, an SOS IM6 built in 1931, was fitted with a Short body and loaned to the War Department for a period. Next to it is KPT 280, a postwar single-deck Guy Arab 5LW with Brush bodywork.

Below right: Durham City bus station showing three different vehicles with three different operators — an AEC Regal of Northern General, a Bristol of United and a Leyland Tiger of Sunderland District a subsidiary of Northern General.

Left: Nearby in Newcastle wartime Karrier JVK 280 was dewired, one of the main hazards of trolleybus operation. The extreme angle of the trolley boom is due to the fact that if the booms had been placed back on that part of the wiring where they had left, they would have been put on a dead section.

Below left: Gateshead and District BCN 614 was a Guy Arab III with Park Royal body built in 1950. This company, a BET subsidiary, operated trams up to August 1951 when, using both Guy Arabs and Leyland Titans, it converted to motorbus operation. At one time consideration was given to the use of trolleybuses, in conjunction with Newcastle Corporation, but this scheme never materialised.

Above right: Darlington Triumph sold to BTC and became one of the constituent companies of Durham District. This was formed in 1950 as an attempt by the BTC to reorganise the publically-owned bus undertakings on a regional basis. VR 9810 was one of the earlier vehicles in the fleet, being a Crossley Eagle with Crossley body built in 1931 and acquired by Darlington Triumph in 1935. It is seen in Middleton-in-Teesdale.

Right: OK Motor Services based on Bishops Auckland still maintains an extensive network of services. One of the earlier vehicles in the fleet was UP 5074, a Thornycroft seen at High Force with its spectacular falls of the River Tees some five miles north-west of Middleton-in-Teesdale, one of the more remote termini of OK which is nowadays much more of an urban operator.

Below: GNE Motor Services, owned by G. E. Brown & Son of Darlington, provided a daily service between Darlington and Carlisle, using among other vehicles this standard Duple-bodied Bedford OB, HHN 980.

Cumberland Mints and Lancashire Hotpot (and a little more)

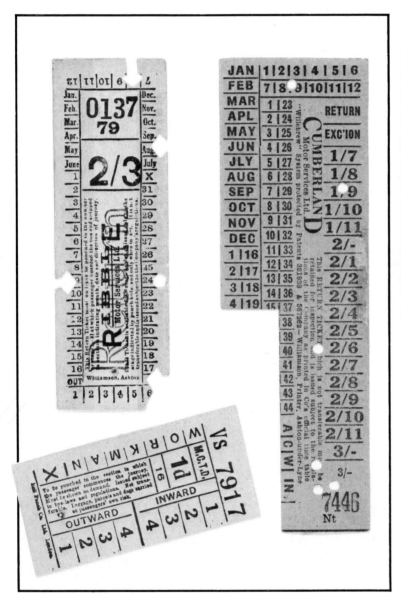

Above: Based at Penrith, E. Hartness operated a number of stage services and developed his business markedly to cope with wartime traffic. This included the use of a small group of double-deck vehicles, concentrating on Daimlers as seen in this view. Operations ceased in 1971.

Left: Cumberland Motor Services came into existence in 1921 after British Automobile Traction had purchased an interest in March 1920 in the Whitehaven Motor Service Co Ltd. This was retitled and services were developed throughout much of the country. The company passed to the Tilling organisation in 1942, but continued to purchase mainly Leyland vehicles until acquisition by BTC in 1948 when Bristol chassis comprised most new deliveries. FAG 282 (23), a Bedford OWB, was one of the wartime acquisitions — arriving in 1944 — and is seen here at Buttermere en route for Cockermouth.

Above left: Whitehaven bus park in April 1955 including the rear views of GAO 308, a Leyland Tiger PS1, and GAO 764, another Leyland Titan PD1.

Below left: Representing the Leylands in the Cumberland fleet is GAO 766, a Titan PD1 with Northern Coachbuilders lowbridge bodywork delivered in 1948. It was one of a large batch of such vehicles delivered during the early postwar years.

Top right: Standing in Keswick is a Bedford WTB of T. Young who traded as Borrowdale Service and worked on the service to Seatoller jointly with three other operators. One of these (Weightmans) was bought by Cumberland in 1958 when the others — Askew, Simpson and Young — formed Keswick-Borrowdale Bus Services Ltd, which passed to Cumberland nine years later.

Centre right: Ribble began in 1919, being absorbed by British Automobile Traction a year later and expanded considerably to cover an area from Manchester, Preston and northwards to the Lake District. An extensive express network was developed, enhanced by the acquisition jointly with Midland Red and North Western of W. C. Standerwick, a coaching company based in Blackpool. Service 667 running between Ambleside and Dungeon Ghyll represents Ribble in the Lake District, seen here operated with a Leyland Cheetah new in 1936 and fitted with Brush bodywork.

Right: Two of the fleet of Leyland Cubs with which the Magnet (C. Head) maintained a frequent service between Windermere station and Bowness pier.

Left: This particular Leyland Cheetah, RN 8050, had Burlingham bodywork and was built in 1937. It was photographed outside the Red Lion at Grasmere.

Below left: A bus station scene at Blackpool during the 1930s showing Leyland Titans of Scout, Blackpool Corporation and Ribble, a Lion PLSC of Blackpool and a Tiger and a Cheetah of Ribble.

Bottom left: Another view of Blackpool, prewar and at high tide. Centre-entrance vehicles were favoured for many years. This example is FV 3562, a Leyland Titan TD3 with Burlingham bodywork.

Right: Lining out was a common feature during the more halcyon days of buses as seen on this immaculate Ribble Leyland Titan TD5 of 1938 vintage and equipped with lowbridge bodywork by Brush.

Below: One of the famous Ribble White Lady vehicles, DCK 221, a Leyland Titan PD2/3 with East Lancs coachwork working limited stop service X13 between Manchester and Great Harwood.

Above left: Preston, in the heart of Ribble operating territory. The rears of Leyland Cheetah RN 8021, with Eastern Coach Works body, and RN 8302, a Leyland Titan TD5, are seen in the Tithebarn Street bus station where nose-on loading was standard practice.

Left: Scout Motor Services was for many years an independent concern although it worked very closely with Ribble on a small group of local services in the Preston area as well as express operations, mainly between Blackpool and London. Leyland vehicles dominated the fleet. Seen in Starchhouse Square, ARN 951 (29) was one of two Leyland Titan PD1s with Leyland lowbridge bodywork delivered in 1946. The other bus, FTE 568 (7) a wartime Guy Arab, belonged to Bamber Bridge Motor Services.

Above: Preston was the meeting point for a number of independents. At the Fox Street bus station, independent operator, J. Fishwick & Sons of Leyland, Lancs, provided a service to its home town with what else but Leyland Titans! The service indeed continues.

Above right: CK 4610, a Leyland Lion belonging to Viking Motors (Preston) Ltd, seen standing in Starchhouse Square while working a route to Woodplumpton.

Right: Two small boys, one with essential rations in the form of Tizer, stand at the entrance to an AEC Regal IV with Burlingham 44-seat bodywork which was acquired by Lancaster Corporation in 1957. The vehicle and three others were new to Rochdale in 1953.

Above: A number of operators employed mobile canteens for crew relief purposes. GKA 288 is one example owned by Liverpool Corporation. Like others it shows traces of a British scheme for articulated buses hatched during the war.

Below: Liverpool Corporation in postwar years employed large fleets of AEC Regents and Leyland Titans, many of which were purchased to replace trams. At the Pier Head terminus is RKC 256, a Titan PD2/20 bodied by Alexander.

Above right: Birkenhead may have been the birthplace of trams, but they did not last after 1937 when Leyland Motors was providing most of the Corporation's rolling stock. ACM 108, in its latter days reduced to a training vehicle, was a well-proportioned Massey-bodied Leyland Tiger PS1 built in 1948.

Right: The now-disappeared North Western Road Car Company is represented by JA 7739, a prewar Bristol L5G with Eastern Coach Works bodywork. Like many other vehicles of the period, it was rebodied shortly after World War 2.

Well North of the Border

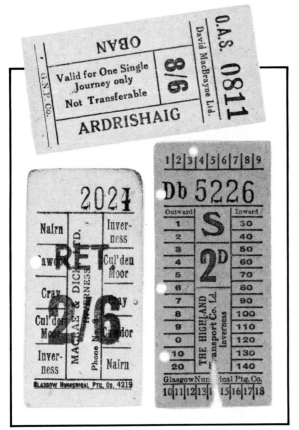

Below: The Greig fleet contained this ex-demonstrator Crossley Condor, VR 8627, seen here in Inverness on the route to Kessock Ferry.

For a look at Scotland, we have chosen largely the Highlands of the past. This was an area where Charles spent a number of holidays resulting in an interesting coverage of such operators as Highland Transport, which in 1952 — together with Macrae & Dick and the Inverness services of W. Alexander & Sons Ltd — formed today's Highland Omnibuses Ltd. The Alexander interest was based partly on the operations of W. Greig who had sold out in 1947. One of the other main operators, David MacBrayne Ltd, had developed both road passenger and freight services as well as steamer services in the Western Highlands and Islands. In addition to holding a Royal Mail contract, the company was one of the few operators to be in receipt of a subsidy for unremunerative services.

Above: An interesting selection in Inverness outside the Macrae and Dick premises shortly after Alexander's takeover of Greig. CK 4869, a Leyland Titan TD3, had been acquired from Ribble by Alexanders in 1947 while behind is BST 53, a 1945 Guy Arab II carrying Greig's fleetname.

Left: This normal-control Albion PK114, ST 8667, with Albion bodywork, was new in 1936 and is seen in Macrae and Dick livery. The vehicle was finally withdrawn 19 years later by Highland Omnibuses.

Below left: Inside the Macrae and Dick garage with, on the right, one of the British European Airways Commer Commandos used on airport feeder services at Inverness, while to the left is the rear of ST 9101, a 26-seat Albion PH115 with body by the same manufacturer, new in 1937 and withdrawn in 1955, having passed to Highland Omnibuses. Facing forward is CS 3895, another Albion PH115 but with Cowieson bodywork, which also passed to Highland Omnibuses.

Above: XS 4409, an Albion SPPW145, was new to Young's of Paisley in 1937 but was later acquired by Macrae and Dick. This bus, which had a 39-seat Cowieson body and also passed to Highland Omnibuses, is seen about to leave Inverness on the long run to Fort William.

Below: In the Highland Transport fleet itself could be found ST 8652 (68) an Albion SPW141 with Cowieson body, but rebuilt by the operator.

Right: Example of Highland Transport double-deckers, BST 571 (51) was a Northern Counties-bodied Guy Arab with Gardner 6LW engine while behind is BST 69 (25) a 5LW-engined Guy Arab with Weymann body.

Below right: While all the previous pictures covered the early postwar scene in Inverness, this view shows a Highland Transport AEC Regal around 1935 with Porteous of Linlithgow bodywork.

Above: A final return to Macrae and
Dick, but in prewar days, who using
GJ 2391, a Chevrolet, previously with
H. J. Phillips and Sons of London,
operated through from Inverness to
Fort Augustus. The service also
continued to Fort William,

Right: No 18 in the MacBrayne fleet
was a Bedford WTB with a 20-seat
Duple body. The low seating capacity
is due to the provision of a mail
compartment, a virtual standard
practice.

Below right: A postwar view of
MacBrayne at Fort William with two
Maudslay Marathon Mark IIIs,
FUS 842 and 841. Both were bodied
by Duple and delivered in 1948.
FUS 841 was later rebodied by Duple
with a full-fronted Vega model.

Above: Typical of the earlier small vehicles used by MacBrayne was SB 3832, a Bedford WLG, new in 1931 with 20-seat Bracebridge bodywork. The fleetname David MacBrayne (1928) Ltd has had the 1928 part crossed through deliberately. The company had been reconstituted in that year by the LMS Railway and Coast Lines Ltd since the original organisation decided not to renew its contract for the mail service, and no other undertaking was able to carry out this work. After some years the new owners were allowed to revert to the original name which they did by showing the 1928 addition had been removed.

Left: This seven-seat Commer with its rather larger tyres belongs to MacGillivray of Dervaig, on the Isle of Mull, which worked on a service to Tobermory where connections were made with the MacBrayne steamer for Oban.

Above left: When bought by MacBrayne in 1958 the Skye Transport Company was among the road passenger interests of the Scottish Cooperative Wholesale Society. Skye Transport had been formed earlier to take over from Highland Transport when that company felt impelled to withdraw. This view of a Ford (ST 7347) at Kyleakin might be said without unkindness to represent a typical prewar scene.

Left: Sutherland Transport & Trading Company operated long-distance services into Lairg from as far away as Durness (57 miles) carrying passengers, mail and goods. Vehicles had to be designed specially for this purpose and Albion ST 2388 was typical of the fleet in the 1950s. The rear had opening doors to facilitate freight handling.

Below: An AEC Regal of Blue Belle, the London coach operator, seen in Pitlochry operating for McKircher of Aberfeldy.

South of the Border

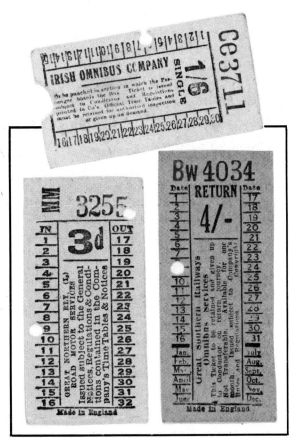

Independence had been granted to the 26 counties of Eire before motor transport had made an appreciable impact on the life of this country. Nevertheless, the British influence continued especially with vehicle purchases, although much of the bodywork was built locally. Bus services mainly in the hands of the Great Southern Railways, which for a time controlled and subsequently absorbed the Irish Omnibus Company, developed slowly because of the rural nature of the country.

In 1945 the GSR was merged with the Dublin United Transport Co Ltd in the state-owned transport undertaking, Coras Iompair Eireann (CIE). One other important concern, the Great Northern Railway — GNR (I) — operated and maintained extensive bus services in Eire until 1959 when the company, facing serious financial problems, was absorbed by CIE and the Ulster Transport Authority.

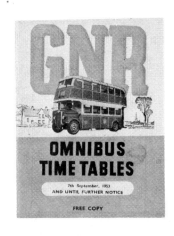

Left: A Leyland Titan TD1 delivered to the Irish Omnibus Company in 1931, complete with 51-seat bodywork to Leyland design, but built by the Great Southern Railways. No 803 (PI 6052) was delivered for use on the Cork City Services to replace the tramways, eventually passing to CIE it was withdrawn in 1947.

Below left: This 1938 Leyland Tiger TS8, ZC 3749, was photographed in Macroom, en route from Killarney to Cork, in Great Southern Railways livery. Bodywork was by GSR. A very typical rural scene for the 1930s with an absence of motor traffic and the domination of bicycles as the supplementary form of transport to the bus.

Above right: Photographed at the old CIE bus terminus in Parnell Place, Cork, this 1948 Leyland OPS3, ZD 7166 with 39-seat forward entrance bodywork by CIE, waits to depart for Crosshaven.

Right: PI 6692, a Leyland Lion LT6, was new in 1934 to the Great Southern Railways and is seen here some years later in CIE ownership outside the Tralee garage.

Below: Leyland vehicles were popular both with the GSR as well as Dublin United Tramways, which, from 1937, purchased many both as tram replacements and to expand the public transport network in the capital. This Leyland Titan TD5 entered service in 1939 with a 56-seat body constructed to Leyland design by Dublin United. Behind is one of the Leyland Lions (ZA 3855) also bodied by Dublin United.

Below: The Great Northern Railway of Ireland, apart from building its own vehicles with Gardner engines, purchased a number of AECs, represented by this 1948 AEC Regal III, with a body by Park Royal, but completed by the GNR(I). In 1959, on the demise of this railway, the vehicle passed into the ownership of the CIE. Behind it is one of railway's AEC Regent double-deckers.

Bottom: The rear of three Great Northern Railway-built vehicles. ZD 727 and 724 were constructed in 1941 and IY 6184 with more angular lines arrived eight years later. Both chassis and body were to GNR(I) design. These are seen in the depot adjoining Donegal station on the narrow-gauge County Donegal Railway, which was partly owned by the GNR(I).

A Brief Excursion into the Six Counties

In 1935 a government organisation, the Northern Ireland Road Transport Board (NIRTB) took over all road transport in the province, including those of the GNR(I) running wholly within the six counties, with a duty to co-ordinate operations with rail services. This did not materialise: the other railway-owned buses were absorbed into the NIRTB and competition increased. Whilst this was soon recognised, war postponed action and indeed with the extra traffic on offer gave the railway network a reprieve, but in April 1948 the Ulster Transport Authority was created to take over both NIRTB and the railway. The aim was to operate a completely integrated transport system. The results were railway closures and the continued dominance of the bus.

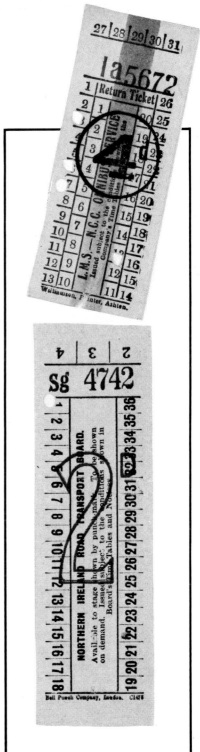

Below: The NIRTB inherited a variety of vehicle types, but during the war faced a considerable increase in traffic requiring the acquisition of a large number of Bedford OWBs. GZ 2479 was in fact delivered at the end of hostilities in 1945 being fitted with standard 31-seat Duple bus bodywork. Parked close behind is a lowbridge double-decker of NIRTB probably one of the few Guy Arabs in the fleet.

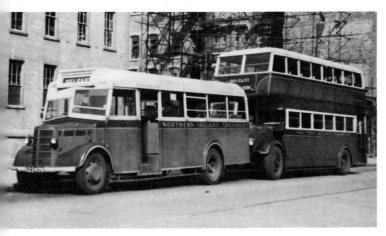

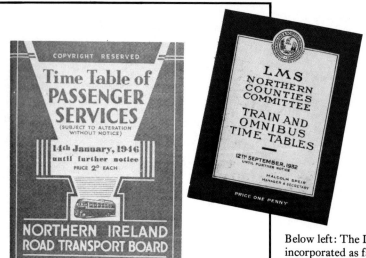

Below left: The Londonderry and Lough Swilly Railway incorporated as far back as 1853, first entered the bus business in 1929 and thereafter progressively replaced train services with road transport. Based in Ulster but with the majority of services operating in Eire, the company had its fair share of problems, both political and financial. Vehicles and staff had to be licensed in both countries. In this scene, a 1949 Leyland Tiger PS2/1 with Ulster Transport Authority 34-seat bodywork is standing at Malin Head, the most northerly bus terminus in Ireland and although situated in the Republic was normally reached through Derry. The star on the radiator is purely unofficial but was the pride of the driver.

Below: Photographed when new in June 1934, this diesel-engined 32-seat Metropolitan Cammell-bodied Leyland Tiger TS6, CZ 4815, was part of an order to the Northern Counties Committee of the LMS Railway which operated some of the main railway lines in the province. The vehicle became M416 in the fleet of the NIRTB.